This
Leaving
We Cannot
Live
Without

This
Leaving
We Cannot
Live
Without

Poems by
Judith McPheron

This Leaving We Cannot Live Without

Poems by
Judith McPheron

Corona Publishing Company

San Antonio

1985

CORONA
Publishing
Company

Library of Congress Catalog No. 84-46169
ISBN 0-931722-34-9

ACKNOWLEDGMENTS

Acknowledgment is made to the following publications for poems which originally appeared in them.

Artful Dodge: "Cancer V," "Cancer VI"
Cincinnati Poetry Review: "The Old Lady to Her Granddaughter"
Connecticut River Review: "For the New Year, 1979"
Cypress Review: "The Fruits of the Earth"
Harper's: "Water" from "Mending the Circle"
New Mexico Humanities Review: "Forty Wing March"
Poetry Dallas: "A Note on Eggs"
Sarcophagus: "A Woman Braiding Her Hair, Saturday"

CONTENTS

These Branches, These Trees

Porchlight, plum blossom, the green
glider pushing through folds of air:
it is easiest to remember branches,
caught in the slipknot of spring,
snagged with regret.

Small breeze fluttering curtains
in the open windows, my father's house
in a thicket of trees, drifting all night,
swelling in the boned air.
These branches belong to the trees of the dead.
There are stars buried in the roots
of these trees, waiting patiently
in crosshatch and murmur, ancestors
shaped like five-fingered hands, waiting
still to take hold of the air, waiting to shine.

Room

If I had my way, you
would be sitting in the other
room, rocking a spare
wooden chair; and when
you whistled (you do
know how) birds would flutter
up from your moving
lap and out the windows.

I sit with head bent over
a mossy cup of tea,
reading the steam, thinking
about chambers,
passageways, the trip,
inevitable as
a winding ball of twine,
to the other room.

Renaissance

This lesson is the first one:
breathe in, once, and it
leaves you.
You stare at the mountain
and nothing is wrong.
In the cold stream your feet
are gelatinous.
The air is metallic —
skin of fish.
The story is the one about
living in a whale's stomach.
If you could plant your seeds
in there.

You want to lie on a bench
in the sun without moving.
Each drop of water
on your skin demonstrates
the lesson slowly:
evaporate, evaporate.
You want to float in the light
between yourself and the bench,
warming into stillness,
breathing still, against the current.
The sun curves over the bench,
over all the little silver fish,
this is summer vacation,
your first summer vacation,
the air is shining
very still and very close.

Late Blooms

Pomegranate blossoms, flaming, not seemingly
contained by natural boundaries
cross my mind, but they
do not illuminate it. It is a foggy
day, my mind will not clear enough
to permit thought or color
to enter and I have recently
learned that I will die.
A branch of flowers so delicate
only defines itself through
slow movement, connections
to the other branches, the white stucco
house it poses in front of.

Focus

You say you are obsessive:
well then, concentrate on
the small bone above
my wrist. It forms
a valley, a congregation
of innocence and little flesh.
Once the soft bone
of a young girl, spongy space
to fill and test the world,
now there is flex
and stopping when you
single out this bone.
Skin, only a tarp
to deflect light, circles
a sherd of agility,
a shattered bit of repose.

You say you love excess:
this is such a place
of procession and rest.
Filaments, cords,
carriers of liquid and
less mystery, it all adds
up to at least a tough flicker.
What holds you holds you well
I'd guess.

What I Know About You Now: for my parents

Today I received a picture
of you on the beach.
Overexposed: too much
light, too much skin.
I think I would
not see you this way:
white as chickens, small,
plucked.

Jamaica, Ma, Dad, a straw
hat, palm tree, and so
white, I want to yell
at you cover up,
cover your teeth
at least.
The brightness leaches
the colors of you
till you are almost back
fifty years, to
black and white.

Only when I insisted
on knowing
the beginnings of you,
you made up a story:
the beach, Brooklyn.
Even then you meant,
ha, this
you'll never know.

I imagined a great heartbreak
for you, Ma—
a young man walking
the boardwalk, with sand
between his toes.
He dropped the ocean
in a mailbox and left
you home.
Each year a postcard
of Atlantic City,
on the mantle,
fades a little more into
a brown and salty
replica of itself.
You settled on Dad instead.

So now it's as if all this
water and sand and light
were a vindication.
You hold hands
on a beach far away
from me, melting
your palms to a picture.
You are the postcard
sent home to me.
You love this day
and make it fast:
grinning and disappearing
in the snapped up sun.

Rising and Falling

It is a song that glides
through you.
You are a thin child
standing still singing.
On very thin legs, bird
legs your Daddy said
must be good for something,
you stand on a sidewalk
in autumn startled
by the clean things
moving out of your mouth.
It doesn't matter
that you feel your tongue
darken and separate
from your throat: you sing
like a bird flying
away from its only nest,
flying away for winter
for good through the rustling leaves.
It doesn't matter why
the song picks you,
its opening out into beauty,
or how you can stand
the refusal of perfection
in every bright falling leaf.

Angel or *bird*, it doesn't matter:
these are the clear rising
words that fly as I speak
them, to you, little wing,
little promise, to you.

Harvest, Fall 1978

I dreamed that as we sat around
a campfire, we all grew fur.
Not slowly at all. You asked me
what kind and I couldn't answer.

We sat on a fence cradling rabbits
in our arms. It was their
ears that most delighted us.
Some stood up, some flopped.

A blind man in a black suit spoke
to me in my dream. He spoke Spanish
and I understood. He only cared
for a sick dog, but I
didn't mind.

Four dead fish form a rough square.
Two lie flat with their
noses pointing in, and two
arch away. In the center is
a codex bird with terrifying
wing span.

The ripple in the glass
means that it was made by
hand, or long ago, or
that it is not perfect.
Not equal weights, but
gestures just the same.

Back and Forth

All night you tunnel
through me as you sleep.
You hold tight to your
edge of the bed, terrified
of backing into absence.
When you turn and grab
me, you say,
with disgust, only animals
move into each other
while they sleep.

Being a scared animal
in a tunnel is not
so terrible, I say.
There are lights, sometimes,
walls, places to stop
and rest.

Terrible enough, you say.

The Fruits of the Earth

You are astonished
and I am tired.
You say this
and sigh.
We have shared
the kindly fruits of the earth;
what is so difficult?

You think a woman
in a red dress,
a woman with arms so long
and supple they could reach
around and cradle the world,

let her be kind,
let her
let me know
This is enough.

Each nod of my head
is a joke
with the punch line missing.
Having eaten and talked
and slept with you, wanting
so much, like you,
to lie down
in a kind bed that murmurs
I'll never let you die,
I unfurl:
a weary seed
in the hard ground.

Cancer I

Is cancer a
violent revolution or
the ebbing of the tide
I wonder as I stare
at the acoustical-tiled ceiling
trying to erase
the insistent pattern there.

Blood or salty water
it's all the same
to me
my bones reply.

Cancer II

Something always grows
from nothing.
To name a lump
is to distinguish
something we wish
were still nothing
to give it shape
and almost
the status
of a piercing organ.
(Who, really, eats
liver without wincing?)
Ah, but a lump
growing willy-nilly
doing things
even when we sleep.
I relinquish control
but do not want
to stop knowing
the names of things.
And it is curious,
yes, like words
we can't imagine
once they grace
the formerly empty
piece of paper
that something grows
from nothing.

Cancer III

Christ in heaven,
there is no reason
to pull the dark
from your sleeve:
I maintain a silence
of a different order.

If my insides speak
a clotted language
all their own,
I am privy only
to a catcall.

Birds, bats, glassy-eyed,
with what passionate resignation
do they beat their wings,
dazzling the ground
with their frenzied noise.
I see them I hear
them apart and above
as I join the
surfaces of the deaf.

Cancer IV

What I know is
we wake to the world each day
children, porcelain.
Such tiny hands,
such delicate bones
the newly risen have.

There is a trace of
well-bred civility
in these proportions
in the white shirts and
milk teeth that grace
the air about the
almost gotten-up.

To lie down with the small
seems less a matter of choice,
more an instance of being caught
with one's bloomers in the breeze.
We grow large, yes,
and coarse
when there is no
getting out of bed.

Cancer V

Twelve fingers, I counted
twelve fingers this morning.
I grow extras
by means of wit or whimsy
and sometimes love extravagance.

Petunias need
watering and tending
to grow
and automobiles need spare parts
just to stay the same
but I elaborate
on an unknown formula
for something like
spontaneous combustion.

I wonder if piano players
would envy me;
I watch as extra things appear
like scum
on a winter's sea.
They multiply
without a backward glance
at the tables.

There should be
a more comfortable spot
for will here,
and precision;
for the sensible rhythm
of note following note.
What I see and hear
makes me bow my head
and echo, simply, there is not.

Cancer VI

At no time did
I expect what I found:
ordinary ecstasy.

I am aroused by
drudgery and carloads
of work brought to fruition.
I quiver when I see
carefully tended orchid plants
in the hands of others.
What is found on
my plate pleases me and
I sleep with ease at
the appointed hours.
Do not mistake this
condition for timidity.

Do not come to sing
for me
at the wailing wall.

Fish Lovers

Time turns us to fish
and teaches us to avoid predators.
Nothing barbed or hooked
can snag us
for we swivel and shimmy
our silver-sided
flesh away
and through the salty water.

Sediment of old
fish bones and
chips of shell
bits and pieces of
tarnished metal
conspire to bed with us
where they can.

I will wave you
through layers of silt
and moving water
swim with you
to the surface where we can breathe.
Curve of fins
curve of scales,
describe your perfect arcs
upon our journey.
We are darting in and out
of love, and
all the webbed reaches
of the sea
move us to
translucent endings.

Horticulture

The paper in the fortune
cookie reads thus:
'God has given you one
face and you make yourselves
another.'
In this room, there are
roses, dark petals on
the lids of a dead man.

My father said *rosebud*
when I was born, for my
mouth, the petaled fragrant
thing he saw and knew he
had no hand in.
From his mouth to mine,
that word
in essence vegetal.
Flowery daughter, petal red,
her first face a gift,
God's pinkest offering
shy of blood.

Make yourselves: so we did,
father, daughter,
interlopers with awe
in our hands.
I pulled my father's
mother's face, lines and seams
into the light
through my own mouth
and skin and eyes,
wrought them into a semblance
that he could see
and call resemblance.
The second face is craft,
not sweetly given bloom.

Now in this room flowering darkness
a man laid out with roses
on his eyes comes to his third
and loveliest face:
petals of deepest red
on a still white field.
Fullness and shadow cast
in proportion I do not want
to think we share,
cast without secrets,
this is not anybody's
father, or, yes, anybody's father,
daughter, son;
pure art,
the final incarnation,
the face of what
we all become.

A Woman Braiding Her Hair, Saturday

Six channels of hair
divided by two
move along the edges of her body.
She sits, paler than
the clumping snow
just outside
watching herself, benign,
in the moon-shaped mirror.
Braiding some white
hairs, too,
the fingers show
no signs of regret.

Mending the Circle

Fire

Grass dreams its own fire
at the end of summer.
Not a flame dance or
a circle of tongues licking blades,

this is a dream of opposition:
red against the absence of green.
Smoke follows grass in a burning field
like the scent of loss and loss annealed.

Water

There is always a journey
to the sea, friend.
Put my bones in a good jar
for the salt is very hungry

and I want to rest
a while on the water.
Waves, like the cool white hands
of my dreams, lift me, carry me home.

Earth

Roots reach worries in this earth
as fat and white as grubs.
These are the secrets we want to keep
preserved, in the yellow clay of a ginger jar.

Out of the jarred night, out of a crater
in the earth, we ask to be born, root children
plowing against gravity, with the sweet taste
of each little death searing our mouths.

Air

Every day our breaths untangle in us
like long hairs being laid to rest.
Fierce rest: our lungs combing
clean the knotted edges of the air.

And beyond the edges, the stars,
those little siftings of pain
lighting up the darkness—
they remain, and ask to be remembered.

Animal

Before we were fish
flipping in our own salt dark,
Before we were bears on four feet
with fur as thick as forest leaves,

Before we were birds rocking forward to sore light,
the first bones of our fins and paws and wings held
and dropped like hands
one by one into our deep and open graves.

Vegetable

In these old shoes I go out to pick pomegranates.
As I reach through the green leaves, my hands
displace the memory of pollen in the warm air.
This is the revenge of the harvest.

I think they try hard to hold on to the tree.
Their bright skins, so beautiful, are turning
to new leather. So much is leaving in me,
splitting apart, like red fruit, ripe, and full of seeds.

Mineral

'Stone is virtue,' says the final flesh
in its cold feathers. This is true
as the wind is true, moving
through snow on the side of a mountain,

unsettling its own powdery name.
We wait to become the stillness of stone.
Snow dust and crystal, dissolute, seeping
into the spare white ribs of rock: we shiver, we wait.

Dream

Night surrounds the gestures it can't quite contain—
light leaning through smoke,
the shined space between two hands, unfolding,
the tiny stick at the center of each cell.

All around me the day is rising
as ghosts rise, effortless, from the grave,
lifting me like a curled leaf asleep on the water,
gathering me to its *lean*, *shine*, *stick*, letting me go.

Space

Let us pretend, or agree to
try, that it is not notions
that stand between us.
Spools of thread, you gloat.
I read about a mass failure
of the will in every other magazine
I sample but the only time you
couldn't get it up was when
you left your wife.
You would say, I'd guess, that
nothing stands between us,
extravagance is merest necessity,
and in all things we
might as well claim perfection
or at least something slippery.
When I want to tell you this,
you press my breasts
with your breath and
an almost unbearable warmth covers me.
I don't much like it,
having been trained for such
a long time to think
of myself as cold.
Your hands with nails so
beautiful they make me blink follows
your breath because
you are bent on destroying
whatever ideas I have of myself as
well as the dissolute,
agreed upon
space between us.

Contingency and Dialectic: a Conversation

Between push and pull
there is something easy.
A woman and man sit on the bed
rocking and their heads
are moss-covered stones.
Like trout whose colors
inform us only as they move
through water also moving,
the bed rocks till they
think their backs
are free of bones.
I'd like to say that
moments accrue, and though
they fall away, accrue again.
Only a tree rooted
by the river or a bird
sailing the weather,
each returning the thoughts
of a lifetime, would hear me,
and testify.

For My Friend with Hair

Once, I was so moved by your
hair, the even, quiet abundance
of it, moving alone, into
braids on a snowy day, that
I wrote you a poem. See how
I mistake you for your hair?
Now, you have had it cut, frizzed,
whipped into style.
I prepared for a profound
disappointment, and it is true that
the result is pretty but
ordinary, fluffy, a circle of feathers one
might want to touch but never a substance
to inspire distance, radiance,
gratitude. And yet you
remain singular.
When you explain to me why a
gesture attracts you, I
see you across the table and
am reluctant to deny the power of
the physical. If you
do not reside in hair, face,
fingers chopping the air,
then it is hard for me to
know where to look.

Tornado

A tornado is a way
of focusing attention
on a point of stillness.
Which is to say
a tornado is discrete
a part of nothing else
not natural
nor supernatural either
an event
which creates no memory
for itself
which shapes time
to itself.
The newscaster asked the old man
whose house was just blown down
in a tornado
(they have no names like Flora, Dora and Sally)
Well, have you ever seen anything like this?
expecting him to say "No,"
this is like nothing
I ever seen,
but he said Oh yes, seen them all.
The cement shelter shook
and belied its heavy weight
a light thing ready to fly away
it oozed a warmth of radios
and blankets
and people who touched their hair
with their hands
just to make sure it was there
and waited
relaxed in the wet comfort
to be marked and held
for a moment
before moving on.

Husband

Each morning, outside the east
windows, the birds squawk furiously,
recalling me to my life, willing
to sell my secrets for a nickel
to the first person who asks.
Is that what you call the abstract
prerogative? I have
a small lump in my throat
right now.

You think it's another story,
but I know better.
Our telephone lines connect
in black and buzz
all along my lit-up veins.
I whisper tender things
at the mouthpiece, and
fish swim out your end,
glittering their fins
for all they're worth.
Boundaries, ah, if only
you'd asked, were never
my intention.

A Note on Eggs

I wanted to say to a friend
well you can't die with me so
why should I go eat scrambled
eggs with you?
At that moment I knew why
people have always attributed
great power to ghosts.
Such rippling hands, my
friend has, such
a way of holding
the hairs on his head.
And I remember what I've
always known, that
the right activity for human
beings is making distinctions.
He said to me in a voice I
mistakenly thought aloof
at least I'll walk you to the door.

Naming the Rain

All evening, I've been staring
through the channels
in the leaves
swelling outside my windows,
waiting for a storm.

The color of light, tentative,
the screens shimmering in the haze
of heat, the dark leaves
floating in the liquid air:
like happiness,
I resist them.

Like thunder, I
insist upon distance.
Lightning cracks
at the edge of the room
and we heave into rain
relieved, as if this were
a little wooden boat
set out, finally, for deep waters.
We list and rock in
the rain, feel our painted sides
splinter like shooting stars
and let go.

All around me the black trees
hold out their heavy limbs
beckoning me, flesh to flesh,
and I almost grab one.
I turn and pull into the weather
toward the open channels
shouting *Lord, God, Terrible*
Is Thy Name
in the empty space
at the top
of my lungs.

For Those Who Dug Potatoes

My relatives, be with me
tonight.
I dream that you dig
potatoes as I sleep,
the grubs climbing
your yawning fingers.
Your lives are ciphers,
small, twisted, the scaly
layers turning around
in the dark of endless
fields. Uncles, aunts,
you hold a stone for me
in one hand, a potato
in the other, and
you are ready.
What you hurl at me
I receive, and
call it nourishment.

Poland. Three men in black coats
stamp around a brush fire,
with hot potatoes
in their pockets.
They stop themselves in dreams
because no one's life
is like a field: large,
flat, and fertile.
They rock on their heels
and sigh through their teeth;
to a child, the sighs
are pleading—
harbor me, harbor me.
It is just seed,
sailing through a place
where a tooth was and out
into the wind.

My relatives, innocent
of America, dig potatoes
before I am born, and cut
each eye carefully,
hoping for propagation.
Comfort comes from clean hands,
imagined at bedtime.
Comfort comes when each dreams up
his own New World.

One uncle thinks another's
pockets are bulging.
I swear, brother, I would
kill you for the eyes of these potatoes
you steal.
And his wife tells her heart
to be still, and
stares at the round white flesh
of her hands.
I swear, brother, I would take you
and slice you
apart, and the light
in you would flicker away.

Smudge fires are for the plants,
young plants, and bugs
are picked off by hand,
a dying art, as they say.
Hot potatoes in your shoes,
rags, papers, make you dance.
The big fine tubers
are for the sacks, not
anyone's pockets, toes.
The big ones, as everyone
knows, are winking beauties.

Be with me tonight, I cannot bear
the weight of this
New World alone.
Be with me, you who know
how to sigh in the filth of fields,
and carry your comfort,
round and hard, into the night.
Be with me, flesh
and layered flesh, because
you know, beyond doubt, that
those who believe
death is a noun
are mistaken.

Forty Wing March

Twenty grey pigeons smudging
through the spring air
know more of home
than I do.
It is roofs, they tell me.

What a comfort to
be a carrier, not cargo;
diseases pre-dating urban blight
nestle among matted feathers as
they cluck and pick
and waddle their ways
through the soot.

I mean that
they have a talent for intimacy.
I do not think
that is romantic projection
for who wants to cozy
up to a pigeon
or wear such dilapidated
feathers in his cap?
Again, I mean
what a certain bird contaminates
is only what is
left over and up
and, surely, its own.

Twenty grey pigeons is
not, after all, an army
of birds. I come
home to a place on top
of nothing, fit a tarnished
key through a screen, and
sigh to shut out
all the missing, feathered world.

The Words We Love

We are sitting at the kitchen table,
talking about the word 'character.'
It is someone else's father who grew
corn to cut down locusts
and break open the prairie;
razor rows to stand off
the dust and carve an ornate horizon.

Our fathers, stillness stinging
their dark throats, could find
a corner in any cornfield.

All the fathers would say we
talk too much.
What can we answer them but ourselves?

How can we save the words we love?

The Old Lady To Her Granddaughter

You think your heart
is filled with light.
I could count the rays
on my fingers.
What you need is
a man to buy you
everything.

There is a lark
in your garden, singing
about transcendance.
I answer him
this way: even if
your heart is gold,
I'm bleeding.

You think this
is about death.
You think too much
in this meager light.

Christmas, 1978

Birds' wings rust at
the rim of the earth and
nothing dips below the lit-up
edge of things:
it is solstice, the
quietest day of the year.
Limbs hold
and water frees
itself of massive burdens;
boulders fall away
from sides of mountains
and touch dissolves
into hesitation:
wait for us, it is
the shortest day of the year.

For the New Year, 1979

I am going to ask you to grieve
for a tree.
It is down in the street,
splintered by the side of the railroad track,
pulped quickly in night flashes,
fingered along open grain.

An old lady with yellow bones, caught in
bed can easily be made to fade away,
a dry leaf, a dry whistle,
but this tree, older than
most old ladies, there is so
much of it, flesh, I am
tempted to say.

The smell of cedar burning, or lining
a closet to keep out moths, that
is not violation, and I
am talking about violation.
To be dense and turgid, menacing
live things with jags
and points, the simple
taking up of too much space;
that's what it's like when
something falls that is
meant to stand.

Someone said but nature
must make way for the new, clear
a place, get rid of
those whose sap is gone.
Filched of grace but not yet
of power, this tree
is taken and the woods will not claim their own.
You are cold, you are
small, your frozen breath spirals
away, and nothing of value
is ever replaced.
Make a noise for it in the thin blue air.

History, a Salty Lick

All loss is salty,
though there is no point
in overstating the case.
The ocean, the deer come out
to lick at the edge of the clearing,
my blood on your door:
each empties smaller
into the next, diminished
and diminishing.

History, love, is boring.
Columbus sailing round
and round the elliptical world,
those hearty pilgrims hacking
a place in the woods,
eating venison and lobster,
quite certain they had permission.
Women, babies, that
salty trail of tears—
is it boring, then, that
each leads me to you?
And though I tear out
my big American heart
and wipe it, ceremoniously,
a gift or taunt, on your
door, my tongue is crusted white;
for all the ships in Christendom,
and then some, will
never bring another wave.

In Response to Roses: For Duane

I find myself a zealot in love
as often as not.
At twelve, the girl who burned
match-book covers for ashes
to wipe on her head
secret Wednesdays
did not know
the transformation
a ceremony of limbs
could work
or that the leavings
of love are almost always
the same.
What marks me does not
wash away
so in between times
when I want to doubt my memory
and call it flatulence
I have only to look in the mirror.
And you, a stranger also to temperance,
read like a tattoo.
We trade lines and smudges,
eager for each sign of ordinance.
What our fingers trace,
our mouths follow,
is it not the detritus of grace?

The Next Step

There is no good time
for a buried life.

I want, I want, I cry
when I wake up in the morning,
but cannot focus on any object.
Taking naps is unbearable.

A facile round of sand
littered with bleached bones
and each one knows my names.
They do not say
how they found out.

Three jars refracting light
stand still and straight
while heavens bound between them.
They tempt me with their casuistry.

Nothing, I tell you,
is as empty as it seems.

Our Glass

Our hands are glass
when we touch each other.
We say moving prisms
to splinter and
contain splinters
but think, really, the green
eye of a Genji dragon,
still, shimmering,
round green glass embedded,
holding and withholding.

I see myself repeated
in your knuckles.
I want to see yourself,
this time, through
my palms, as if
the history of your cells
would come clear
in my hands,
as if this clarity were
disinterested.

Everything between
your centuried body
and my hands makes mirrors.
The air is vectored through
an occasion of light
as we are fields of force
filtering force.
The hands we hold
pour light as wet and luminous
as fear.

You think you want me
whole and round,
glittering eye centered
on you.
A pooling in your palms.
I refract you
off the walls
a thousand times
believing that my fingers
gather you through time.

What we touch
we see shining, burning
our bodies.
In our hands
nothing is old.

Middle Age

You said
in the Middle Ages, green
was the color of hope.
I'm wondering how it is
to lie still under the earth,
my feet picked clean
and sprouting new grain.

In my middle age,
I think of you, the hungry dark,
the early seed
you meant to offer.
I think of the good crumbs
of loam layering over me,
the soft mouths in the crust of soil,
the tiny green flag
I'll fly
in the slippery air.

Yortzeit: Aunt Mary

Tonight the candle in the glass
burns for you, like a hot mouth
sucking a hole in the dark.
It's burned thirty hours, already
longer than it should.

I remember how another night,
you stood in an angry doorway
nodding *too late*.
You told me all the ways
the milk in a woman's breasts
could go sour, then
turned out the light.

In the fading picture,
you crouch, your hand
like a hook on a dog's back,
caught in a shaft of light
twenty years before
I was born.
You remind me of a child.
Oh child, you whispered,
the milky darkness
swallows us all
without our consent.

Now you burn and burn,
impersonal, sweet light
washing my walls.
I can make of your shining
absence a sustenance
or a story, but
not the glassblower's breath
I'd need
to blow
the candle out.

Night Song

You go to sleep each night
trying to re-enact
the pillow.
Sleep.
You will contract
softness bit by bit,
and so compressed,
squeeze us
from the hardness
of our dreams.
Together we may sleep
some twisted thought
away and wake
smooth, like folded sheets,
one inside the other.

Deathsongs

I hear a long word
flying low against its edges.
Every wing that ever
curved through the sky,
fluttered, dropped
on the ground
demands its rightful name.
Listen.

The songs we sing
for the dead are always
losing their words.
New words come quickly,
filling the ground
as leaves do.
They find us, muffle us,
trick us into believing
they were always there.

If we planted a word
in the ground
it would creep the length
of the garden at night.
In each dim window
there might be a face,
in each bed
a sleeper waiting.
Who but the dead
could pick such a word,
hold it,
put it into our ready hands?

2

The air in graveyards
is rich and thick
with the voices of the dead.
Like clabbered cream
holding a spoon,
this air, too, holds us,
upright.
Let these noisy breaths we breathe
nourish us, as they
expand our lungs
with death.

3

Each night as we lie down,
we put on
the faces of the dead.
When we wake,
they are singing.
Our mouths
are long and new.
What word, what
shapely refrain
do they grant us?

4

All my life, I've
been waiting for something
that brushed my face
before I was born.
Sometimes I think
it will be a white sound
ringing through me fast
as lightning.
Sometimes a hand, clenched
in a fist that will
punch me into clarity.
And sometimes a perfect wing arching
out of nowhere,
beating the air around my head,
taking my breath
making me gasp and
cry *mercy, mercy.*

Spirit Song

This flute I'm playing
wakes the insects,
who were sleeping
at my feet.

The plants in the fields
cry all night long
for their cousins.
Even the dew is anxious.

What sounds in the dark
is not some gentle mewing.
It settles, small and wet,
in the folds of our clothes.

There are ladders
in the air, and circles.
What creature isn't
listening, moving?

I tell you, I will not
leave you, though I sing
as you die. I heard this
in a song: pass it on.

31100016

Six hundred fifty copies printed
January 1985